TABLE OF CONTENTS

I

Appendix A: Questionnaire   44

LIST OF TABLES IN TEXT

LIST OF FIGURES IN TEXT

LIST OF ACRONYMS

ADB	Asian Development Bank
BBS	Bangladesh Bureau of Statistics
GNP	Gross National Production
ILO	International Labor Organization
IDPM	Institute for Development Policy and Management
NGO	Non Government Organization
UN	United Nations
UNDP	United Nation Development Program
USA	United States of America

LOCALLY USED TERMS

Chemri   Young female domestic worker
Khalamma   Female employer
Bandha   Permanent
Purdah   Veil
Eid   Main religious festival for Muslim
Ruti   Kind of cake
MA   Mother
Baba   Father

Abstract

This research examines the exploitative situation of female domestic workers in Dhaka, Bangladesh. This study discovers the unfair condition of female domestic workers which place them into higher exploitation in the informal labour market. Domestic workers have, too often, been portrayed as one dimensional victim-a group of powerless women vainly struggling for justice in Bangladeshi society. This research explores how the intersection of gender with class, culture, sex, shapes different experiences for different categories women as employer and employee in domestic service. The research critically asses how the domestic work create an employment sector for poor women of Bangladesh with high level of injustice, insecurity and exploitation. Here this research explores that gender is not the only factor of discrimination against domestic workers. Class and poverty becomes a vital factor in this context. This study unveils how in one hand, the intersectional experience produces authority for upper class women, on the other hand produces domination for the lower class women with in the household of Bangladesh.

Key words: *Labor exploitation, Informal sector, Feminine labour, Female Domestic workers.*

CHAPTER ONE: INTRODUCTION

1.1 Introduction

Employment is still considered as the most reliable vehicle to take the women out of poverty. Labour market is systematically arranged by gender inequality that also reinforces male to hold the formal employment and women to the informal (Sarkar, 2007). As greater numbers of men enter the formal economy, women tend to be pushed to the lowest-income and in the end of the informal economy (Heintz, 2006). However, very little available evidence from surveys across the world suggests that most of the working women are engaged in informal employment which does not usually offer adequate wages, good working conditions and social protection. At the same time, it does not act as a means to get a better and secured life for female workers. Informal sector is a producer of injustice exploitation through incorporate feminine labor (Charmes, 2000). It is found that among all categories in the informal sector, earnings of domestic workers are lowest and their problems are many (Arriagada,1997). Domestic work constitutes an important labor market entry for women. However domestic service is always a last resort occupation. Domestic work is largely unprotected, due to the fragmented and personal nature of employment (IDPM, 2002). Similarly it is also an intriguing occupation. The domestic worker is a part of the household, but not a member of the family. She is hired from the labour market to perform the housework. She performs housework in a private household, her work contribution is considered minimal, meriting substandard wages, and until recently exclusion from protective labor legislation. It can be said that domestic's position performing housework in household as an exploring branch of the informal sector, reinforces her lower status with the high level of exploitation (Pedlar, 1982). This picture is also clear in Bangladesh especially in urban area. Nowadays hiring domestic helper has become a common culture among middle class and upper class household in Bangladesh. This research I conducted to reveals the exploitative condition of female domestic workers in Bangladesh. Moreover this study tries to explore that, to what extend informal structure of the work reinforces the exploitation and exclusion of the female domestic workers in Bangladesh.

1.2 Statement of the problem

In most societies women are employed in domestic service and this practice seen as okay. Bangladesh belongs to a class based society. Most of the vulnerable girl and women from poor

1

household join themselves as a domestic helper. In that context labor market arrangement, gender inequalities and patriarchal ideologies play an important role. Female labour becomes the worst victim of exploitative labor relation. This exploitative situation is stronger in the informal sector. Domestic service still consists in the informal sector as well as the sector of labor exploitation. Due to this manner it can be assumed that that there is a link between working in the informal economy and being poor (Sarkar, 2007). The link between working in the informal economy and being poor is stronger for women than for men (Sarkar, 2007). Informal sector is the strong producer and promoter of poverty as well as financial exploitation for female workers. Poor women are doubly exploited in this situation as well as in the market of informal labour. The situation of female domestic workers in informal sector of Bangladesh understands the cheapest labor. Moreover, Women in this patriarchal sex-gender system, has few capacities to exercise their agency and have few capabilities to barging for better salary (Gerhart and Rynes, 1991). Like most of the countries in the developing world, Bangladesh economies have sizeable informal sectors. Additionally Domestic work is a branch of feminine labor. Women constitute the majority proportion of domestic work. Maximum household of Bangladesh recruits domestic labor and women constitute the highest proportion in this sector. According to the labour survey in Dhaka and Chitagong done by Bureau of statistics, found that 90% of domestic were girls aged 9 to 16 years (Hossain, 2002). These women are trapped in the cycle of exploitation and injustice. They receive a few remuneration and benefit in returns of their day-night services. Female domestic workers are being employed generally for household tasks which include washing utensils and clothes, fetching water, sweeping and cleaning house along with a few outdoor tasks like irregular marketing, grocery shopping, ration drawing, Making endless cups of tea even childcare activity. Going to bed hours after sunset and waking up long before sunrise is the life of many Bangladeshi domestic workers. Typically there age range from age six to twenty, who have little or no access to better remuneration, minimum leave, standard wage scale, bonus, promotion and recreation time.

Domestic workers are employed in private homes to perform household tasks traditionally perceived as inferior or "women's" work. More or less all middle and upper class people in Bangladesh employ preferably female domestic servant in their households. Here the feminine labor is supplied. One of its reasons is availability in low cost labour with less power to exercise agency. The economic compulsion is the main hardship for taking the job as domestic servants. Here domestic work contributes a substantive type of employment and generation of earnings for many women. That is why thousand of women are involving in this sector and contribute a huge labor but receive a little recognizasion of their work. After a day long contribution to household work they are treated as a servant not a worker. In the end of the month they are paid very low moreover experience unlimited injustice thought out the whole month. Female domestic workers are subject to variety of exploitations starting from low wages to maltreatment by the employers. Since they are the labour of informal sector they are easily being exploited by the employers. One of an established fact is that informal sector is a strong platform of gender based inequality which incorporate gender based injustice for female labour (Sarkar, 2007). From very early period informal sector has become a discriminated labor market where female labor suffers the major injustice and discrimination. Government of Bangladesh has taken various initiatives to increase the quality and quantity on female labour force participation by various laws, policies. Recently the government is thinking to increase the period of maternity leave from four to six month. All these initiative has taken for the formal employment. However, these laws and policies ignore a huge number of women engaged in the informal employment. There is no legal protecting and government intervention on the lives of domestic workers who are working behind the closed doors of middle class. This research has given a serious attention to the fact on less concern among researcher and both government and non-governmental bodies in this category of informal labour force. Due to these realities, this study is to reveal the reality and hidden condition of female domestic workers of Dhaka city. In this study it will be analyzed how informal sector produces labour exploitation and insecurity among domestic workers. For this, it will find out the working profile of domestic workers in Dhaka city.

1.3 Background to the study

As the number of female workers in the informal sector in Bangladesh has gone up considerably, it implies employment opportunities for them in the formal sector have become restricted. The female domestic workers have to face many problems at the work place which include low level of wage, a minimal pay or no pay for extra work, absence of leave facility. Because of the private nature of their work, Bangladesh has failed to fully recognize the domestic worker's status as an employee. The issue of gender and informal labor is linked with poverty that has identified as one of the reason behind feminization of poverty. The world's population of poor is commonly estimated at 1300 million (UNDP, 1996). Women, especially in developing countries, bear an unequal share of the burden of poverty; an of-repeated statement in this respect is that 70 percent of the world's poor are women. In Bangladesh Female, domestic workers are in the marginal line in this context. Bangladesh remains a poor country with a per capita GNP 210 US $.naturally the burden of poverty falls heavily on women. Landlessness and extreme poverty creates additional burdens for women in the family. Women's migration from rural to urban is a common expression in this context (Shamim, Huda ,1995). Rural poverty and landlessness push women to migrate to urban household to work as domestic worker. Domestic labour has now become a systematic impersonal exploitation in household (Dogramaci, 1985). The phenomenon of domestic work is not new. Domestic work has existed for centuries in Asia, when girls were sold by poor families to rich ones, put to work as 'slaves', 'maids' or 'servants' or described as a quasi member of the family so as to deny their rights. Today, such feudal and patriarchal values continue to shape the way the work is valued, i.e. it is 'work of no value' done by women of low caste, ethnic group or race. This classification of the work remains unchanged today. Similar situations can be found in Europe, the Middle East and Latin America where the richer class can afford to have a servant, perhaps as a symbol of their wealth.

To understand the context of domestic service in the informal sector we must know the dichotomy between formal and informal employment. It is now widely accepted that such a dichotomy into formal and informal has established. This dichotomy implies that employment in the informal economy is inferior quality compared with formal employment (i.e., no legal minimum wage, no social protection, poor conditions of work, job insecurity, no severance pay, etc. Current thinking on Informal Employment in Bangladesh by Dalisay S. Maligalig, Sining Cuevas and Aleli Rosario (2009) for Asian Development Bank indicates that women constitutes above 91% informal labor force among total number of working women. Recent statistics on sexual composition of employment in Bangladesh is given below.

Table 1: Formal and Informal Employment by sex Estimates, 2005-06

Sex	Total	Percent Employed in	
		Formal Sector	**Informal Sector**
Male	36,079,828	15.40	84.60
Female	11,276,763	8.71	91.29
Total	47,356,591	12.29	87.71

Source:Dalisay S. Maligalig, Sining Cuevas and Aleli Rosario,2009 working paper ADB "Informal Employment in Bangladesh"

Here figure 1 is also showing the sex estimation of employment sector in Bangladesh in the year of 2009

Figure 1:

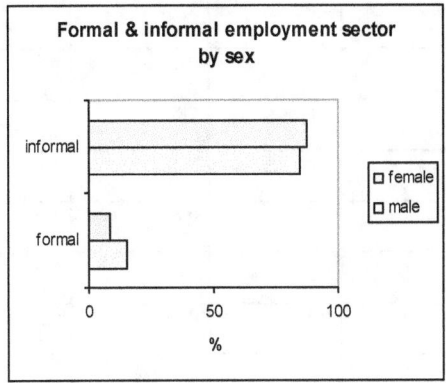

This figure shows that Men outnumber women in the total employed population on a 3:1 ratio. Women are more in number in the informal sector. Here one important fact refers that wheras the highest number of women works in the informal labor marker additionally in that informal market female domestic labor is also highest in number. Feminization of domestic labor had begun in England and France those countries led industrialization in late 1800. The opportunity offered by the factory works in urban centers altered societies and the institution within it. Industrialization and its effect –the changing familial relation, the shift of wage economy and the migration of rural people to urban areas all contributed the exploding of middle class in the urban centers. In that context opportunities of earning a wage were different for a man and a woman. For girls and women domestic service was a job they can performed readily, even no need for special skill, other than what the girl would have learn from family responsibility were required. Still now the sector of domestic labor force is a platform for production of feminine labour as huge number of women works here. Moreover women are also preferred in this labor sector. The number of domestic workers in Bangladesh is increasing day by day. In a research done by Bangladesh Institute of Labour Studies (BILS) and the Social Welfare Institution of University of Dhaka (2010) shows that in Bangladesh 50% of domestic worker's age range in 5-15 year and 76.67% of them are women. Due to women's less capacity to exercise agency, also women are cheap labour and societal perception is that women are for household works they constitute a huge number in this sector than men. Table 2 is giving the evidence.

Table 2: Sectoral Composition in Informal Employment by Sex.

Status	Female	Male	Total (million)
Regular paid employee	1.3	5.3	6.6
Employer	0	0.1	0.1
Self-employed	1.8	18.1	19.9
Unpaid family worker	6.8	3.5	10.3
Irregular paid worker	0.2	0.8	1.0
Day laborer	0.7	7.9	8.6
Domestic worker/maid servant	0.3	0	0.3
Others	0.2	0.4	0.6
Total	11.3	36.1	47.4

Source: 2005-2006 Labor Force Survey, BBS

Bangladesh is a class based society. This study specially focuses here the lower class and the middle class women in Bangladesh. In contemporary society lower class implies the lowest in the social hierarchy who occupy the lowest socioeconomic position in the society. Lower class is a term used in academic sociology and in ordinary conversation to describe those employed in lower tier jobs, as measured by skill, education and lower incomes. On the other hand middle class is a distinct social group with a particular economic bracket cultivated taste, refined behavior, customs, and idealism (Scrase, 2003). Recruiting domestic helper is a trend as well as a culture in Bangladesh. Urban middle class household are the prominent employers of them. Most of the workers belong to very lower class family which makes them more vulnerable to adjust with the newly appointed working condition. . In addition in Bangladesh we belong to the patriarchal society. The patriarchal ideologies roots in the household and explores in the public life, in the market. As well as these patriarchal ideologies restrict women to get the economic benefit in the labor market (Charmes, 2000). Domestic workers who exchange the service they provided for a wage represent a membership in a proletarian class doubly disadvantaged due to their class and gender. They are employed for a better life. Here girl child are treaded as a burden. Even in very early age they are sending by their parents as they could not feed their daughter .These intersecting identities often subject domestic workers to significant hardship in a patriarchal and class based Bangladeshi society. Hence women in domestic service become marginal and deprived in the labor market. From the human poverty or capability perspective women are indeed poorer in most society (Sarkar, 2007). Here domestic workers are doubly

6

exploited first they are a female labor belong to poor family and also they are the labor of informal sector. In Bangladesh the degree of inequality between the employer and the domestic worker can be further stratified by class, gender, and other types of prejudice. Patriarchal capital economy, urbanization and migration also rising women's employment however at the same time these are generating uncertainty for female labors (Selim, 2009). Furthermore female labors are exploited and capitalized in the patriarchal capital intensive labor market since they are marginal and have less capacity to exercise agency to bargain with the labor market.

1.4 Justification of the study

Domestic labour in Bangladesh is a common picture. Thousand of women are employed in domestic service as a social problem resulting from poverty and economic distress of their families. In Bangladesh, urban middle class families cannot think a single day without a domestic helper. The majority of this type of home based workers works in privacy and they are invisible (Sarkar 2007), even not recognized as a worker. Rapid urbanization, migration and especially rapid growth of urban nuclear family have become the strong promoters of employment of domestic workers. I found this sector such as a new area for research. Unfortunately in Bangladesh this study area of gender and domestic service is very much neglected. Number of works has been conducted on the profile of domestic workers in the United State, Europe. But in south Asia, this filed of research has been unfulfilled. Regrettably these issues on domestic service are totally absent in the research filed of South Asia. While domestic service is still a widespread profession for women in South Asia. There are some studies in the context of India but the context of Bangladesh has been ignored where feminine labor is a major characteristic of this sector. My research is a small contribution in this gap in literature.

In the context Bangladesh Nadia Selim (2009) has studied on "Domestic service in Bangladesh a case study in Dhaka where" here she denoted three factors of domestic workers. Personal autonomy, financial security and physical safety were the three dimension of her study on female domestic workers in Bangladesh. Where she said maids are financially secured because they receive housing and food without additional fees. In articulating the situation of female domestic workers in Karachi, Mohiuddin (1982) has investigated the socio-economic aspect of the female domestic workers. He specifically focused on the female-headship in Karachi. In that study the situation of female domestic worker in the labour market has been clearly focused. It has claimed that being a part of informal labour market, domestic work is unprotected. Labour law is not applicable for this sector. This study has expressed the factor of poverty among female domestic workers. Bulgovind Baboo and Laxmi Panwar (1984) have studied the maid servants in Hariana. The study emphasizes that they are leading a miserable life. they examined the suffering of female domestic workers from low wage, long hours of work, shift in nature of job, lack of freedom and low prestige due to inferior status of the job. The fragmented nature of their job, lack of education and low bargaining capacity refrain them from organizing collectively. Asian Human right Commission (2001) has worked on domestic workers. They gave special emphasis on the legal protection of domestic workers in various countries of Asia. This study has been seen from a human right perspective. Another study in United State, by Judith Rollins (1985), claims that the relationship between the employers or the mistress and the domestic worker is the relationship of psychological exploitation. Here she examines the psychosocial determinants of hierarchical social structure. The study "Informal Employment in Bangladesh", done by Dalisay S. Maligalig and Sining Cuevas (2009), found that in the informal economy, employers have the highest earnings and wage workers, the lowest but those self-employed constitute the biggest segment. Huge evidence clears the fact that poverty is a direct link with informal sector (Sarkar, 2007). In the study of Chen (2001) gender perspective has been incorporated in articulating women's employment in the informal sector. It also Most women are informal workers and they are paid less than men of similar class and industry are. Further, and as noted by Chen (2001), there is a relationship between women participating in the informal sector and their level of impoverishment. He also claimed that male informal workers dominate all industry except for personal households.

All these studies have conducted from gender perspective, which argues that domestic service as well as the informal labour market is the sector of gender inequalities. Due to patriarchal ideologies in labour market, Women workers are deprived from their right. These studies have identified gender as the root factor for the injustice and deprivation on female domestic workers. In my study, I want to show that, the injustice and exploitation on female domestic workers in slight different angle. I agree that gender may be a factor but my research tries to explore the game of gender in different way. This study tries to see the domestic service as the sector where the exploitative relation exists in two women. From the intersectional lens this study attempts to challenges the conventional meaning of gender which implies the power relation only between men and women. This research wants to focus on the gender relation between two categories women. One category is the female domestic worker who belongs to the lower class another is her mistress or female employer who belongs to the higher class. In the context of Bangladesh huge works has been done on informal sector for example study has been done on day laborer, construction labor, but unfortunately there is insignificancy in the area of domestic labour force. In the work of the condition of working women of informal sector in Bangladesh, by Karmojibi Nari (2004), emphasis the linkage between informal sector and poverty. In this study domestics service has given few attention where the labor of agriculture, construction, hacker, shrimps cultivator has been given major emphasis. It is true that domestic work is the worst form of labor unit in the informal labor market. None of this study has examined the issue of domestic service as a unique production sector of feminine labor which is a strong perpetrator of labor exploitation. My research want to explain this issue from gender and employment perspective which claims Domestic service is still a strongest branch of informal employment which still promotes feminisation of labour (Chen, 2001). Researches done on feminisation of poverty in the context of Bangladesh have neglected the dynamic aspect of gender and poverty among the female domestic workers. Even the works have done on domestic labor most of them emphasis on the problems of security and safety, working condition, sexual and mental violence rather than the economical exploitation on domestic worker. The factor of growing insecurity and exploitation among domestic workers is untouched. However, the issue of perpetuating economic exploitation by using Feminine labor in domestic service is still untouched; unexamined. This current study tries to unveil the reality of informal labor market as a strong producer of injustice and insecurity with high level of exploitation for female domestic workers. At the same time this study uses intersectional analysis to understand the dynamic aspect of gender relation between two women in domestic service.

1.5 Research objective

This study has given focus on female domestic worker. Over last few decades, there has been a rapid growth in the number of women employed in Bangladesh, while majority of them being engaged in informal sector as domestic worker. Where, they experience high level of injustice and exploitation. The main objective of the study is to find out the ways and strategies by which informal sector produces exploitation for the female domestic workers.

- To Understand Domestic service as the source of exploitation for female domestic workers.
- To find out the intersections in domestic service in Bangladesh.
- To find out the perception of employers toward their employee.

1.6 Research question

The research question I explore is "What are the strategies and factors by which informal sector promotes exploitation among female Domestic workers?"

1.7 Methodology and data collection

The experiences and lives of marginalized peoples, as they understand them, provide particularly significant problems to be explained or research agendas' (Harding, 2005:221). I opt the feminist standpoint theory due to its premises that the evaluation of the dominant institutional practices should be from the standpoint of most marginalized subgroups. Thus, I engaged in this research by taking the standpoint of the marginalized female domestic worker. As Sandra Harding notes that standpoint theory 'requires learning to listen attentively to marginalized people; it requires educating oneself about their histories, achievements and performed social relation' (Harding, 2005:229).

My research is focused on the female domestic workers in Dhaka city. There are mainly two types of domestic workers in Bangladesh. One, Temporary/live-out (Chuta) domestic worker, another is Permanent/live-in (Bandha) domestic worker. My research has been conducted on the permanent female domestic workers. The study is based on qualitative research technique by focusing on a small sample that I can go in the depth of domestic worker's lives and thoughts. The data has collected through in-depth interviews. Observation method is used to get a clear perception of the situation. The research is based on interviews of two sets of people

1. Firstly interview has taken to gather information from domestic workers to know their thoughts and perception and level of awareness towards the exploitation or injustice in their work.

2. In the second step interview has taken from the employers of the domestic workers to analysis their perception towards domestic work, insecurity, and exploitation in their workers.

Various information on seven female domestic workers and seven employers, has gathered from extensive survey of field investigation. The interviews covered a number of issues including family background of the domestic worker, reason to work as a domestic worker. All the interviews have been guided by an open-ended questionnaire. Both grouped women participated in structured interviews which lasted from 45 to 60 minutes. Interviews were tape-recorded with participant's consent.

I have chosen the area of Dhanmondi in Dhaka to interview the domestic workers. Particularly Dhanmondi has been selected as the study place for three reasons. First, Dhanmondi is perceived as one of the living place of middle and upper class people of Dhaka. Secondly, here most of the people live in nuclear family. The trend to employee domestic workers is higher among middle and upper nuclear family. The availability of domestic worker is the reason for preferring the place. Thirdly I assumed the higher level of social awareness and the NGO involvement in this area will make me easy to interact with the domestic workers and their employers. Field visit were carried out over a period of one month. Every participant has assisted with an identification number. Domestic workers working in Middle and upper middle class household has been selected for the study. The age range of the domestic workers is between 12-20 years. Their monthly income is in between 600-1500 taka. The study is based on both primary and secondary data as newspaper articles and Governmental and Non Governmental Organization (NGOs) reports.

1.8 Practical problems in carrying out proposed research

During conducting this study there were some constrains like

- As a researcher I was not cordially permitted to interview the domestic workers.
- There was a tendency to avoid interviews among the employers.
- The employers tried to avoid answering the sensitive question on salaries of the domestic workers.
- Another constrain was domestic worker's unwillingness to answer the question on violence and sexual harassment as they are afraid of losing their job.
- Difficult to get time from working women who are very busy with doing household works.
- Time limitation is one of the most serious problems.

CHAPTER TWO: THEORETICAL FRAMEWORK AND FEMINIST STANDPOINT: ARTICULATING THE DOMESTIC SERVICE

To discover the disadvantaged situation as well as injustice and exploitation of female workers in the informal sector as a domestic_labor this research will explain the theoretical grounding upon which the study is based. The domestic labor debate also serves to illustrate how different women have different everyday realties and how feminist theories have explained or not explained these differences. It will focus on how feminist perspectives explain the strategies of exploitation against female domestic workers in Bangladesh

2.1 The informal economy, arena of interventions: conceptual and theoretical Debates

In this paper, informality is considered in the context of employment. Informality is here defined by the extent to which workers concentrate economic risk (IDPM, 2002). The term informal sector was first initiated by Keith Hart (1970). He describes the informal sector as that part of the urban labour force, which falls outside the organized labour market. The informal economy also has been described as "the economy not covered by official data on registered enterprises" and therefore not registered for the purpose of taxation and or regulation by the state (Harris,White, 2003). ILO (1993) have defined informal sector as, Informal self-owned enterprises which may employ family workers, and employees on an occasional basis, for operational purposes and depending on national circumstances, this segment comprises either all self-owned enterprises, or only those which are not registered under specific forms of national legislation (factories or commercial acts, tax or social security laws, professional groups, regulatory or similar acts, laws or regulations established by national legislative bodies). The term informal economy covers a set of heterogeneous activities, from unpaid labor to any number of unregulated salaried jobs. It also serves the purpose of masking the over-exploitation and socially levered extortion to which the most unprotected and vulnerable members of the working class are subjected (Breman, 2004).

The recent re-convergence of interest in the informal economy has been accompanied by significant rethinking of the concept. In recent years, a group of informed activists and researchers, including members of the global research policy network, Women in Informal Employment: Globalizing and Organizing (WIEGO), have worked with the International Labour Organization (ILO) to broaden the earlier concept and definition of the 'informal sector' to incorporate certain types of informal employment that were not included in the earlier concept and definition (including the official international statistical definition). They seek to include the whole of informality, as it is manifested in industrialized, transition and developing economies and the real world dynamics in labour markets today, particularly the employment arrangements of the working poor. Under this new definition, the informal economy is

12

comprised of all forms of 'informal employment'— that is, employment without labour or social protection—both inside and outside informal enterprises, Including, both self-employment in small unregistered enterprises and wage employment in unprotected jobs. It descries the key feature of the informal economy as following.

Significance and permanence: The recent re-convergence of interest in the informal economy stems from the recognition that the informal economy is growing; is a permanent, not a short-term, phenomenon; and is a feature of modern capitalist development, not just traditional economies, associated with both growth and global integration. For these reasons, the informal economy should be viewed not as a marginal or peripheral sector but as a basic component—the base, if you will—of the total economy.

Segmentation: The informal economy consists of a range of informal enterprises and informal jobs. Yet there are meaningful ways to classify its various segments, as follows:

• Self-employment in informal enterprises: workers in small unregistered or unincorporated enterprises, including:
  o employers
  o own account operators: both heads of family enterprises and single person operators
  o unpaid family workers

• Wage employment in informal jobs: workers without worker benefits or social protection who work for formal or informal firms, for households or with no fixed employer, including:
  o employees of informal enterprises
  o other informal wage workers such as:

    ▪ Casual or day laborers
    ▪ Domestic workers
    ▪ Unregistered or undeclared workers
    ▪ Some temporary or part-time workers1
    ▪ Industrial outworkers (also called home workers).

From recent research findings and official data, two stylized global facts emerge about the segmented informal economy. The first fact is that there are significant gaps in earnings within the informal economy: on average, employers have the highest earnings; followed by their employees and other more "regular" informal wage workers; own account operators; "casual" informal wage workers; and industrial outworkers. The second is that, around the world, men tend to be over-represented in the top segment; women tend to be over-represented in the bottom segments; and the shares of men and women in the intermediate segments tend to vary across sectors and countries. These twin facts are depicted graphically in figure.

Figure 2: Segmentation of the informal sector.

Average Earning   **Segmentation by Sex**

High

Predominantly Male

Rising informality is also associated with reduction   tion arising from welfare reforms. In terms of self-employment, informality is associated with the exclusion of the self-employed from formal social protection program. and their vulnerability to changes in product demand. An approximate measure of Men and Women   ity is the proportion of the labour force not contributing to formal social protection program (IDPM, 2002).

From the perspective of women and employment, a recent rise in the fraction of females in total labor force would suggest that the female labor force is growing faster than that of men. It is widely believed that an increasing share of female employment all over the Predominantly Women

Low

formal but in this informal category (Sethuraman, 1998). Increasing rate of participation of females in the labor market is also reflected in the changing sex composition of the total labor force. Which in reality represent a relatively larger proportion of women than men is believed to be in informal employment. In other words there is a gender bias with regard to the incidence of informality. In comparison to men, a large proportion of women not only receives low returns to their labor but is also exposed to vulnerability (Sethuraman, 1998). The above discussion also shows that informal sector hold a strong segmentation based on gender. Men tend to be consisting in the higher level and women tend to be consisting in the lower level in the structure of the informal labour market. In analysis of the situation of domestic workers feminist have argues that the injustice must be understood as structural rather than cultural (Epstein, 1981 and 1983, Ramirez, 1982, Makeda, 1983, Devan 1989). Whereas domestic service is a branch of informal sector so all the above mentioned oppression and exploitation of informal labour market is more acute for the female domestic workers. The condition of poor women doing domestic work places them in a vulnerable position to become the victim of multiple forms of oppression as they are in the informal labour market. Informal sector is believed as the key producer of feminisation of labour (Chen, 2001). In theorizing the situation of female domestic workers is may articulate that they confined in feminized informal sector. So their powerlessness is due to the nature and the condition of their work which confines in informal sector. Firstly, their work has no specific regulation and policy. Secondly the work they perform is valued as women's work and crates feminine labor which have the minimum wage value. Thirdly, the realities of informal works as domestic workers experience isolation, lack of privacy, lack of option to give any complain against the employers, dependence on employers. These factors are reinforced by the structure of informal economy. The contract system is a common mode of employment across the occupations studied. How it functions, the modes of recruitment, the incidence of harassment and the engagement of the workers with the state are distinct in different occupations. The complicity of the State in perpetuating these systems of informality has had a crucial and adverse impact on urban poverty. Domestic workers are totally excluded from formal contracts paper and documents.

The critical concern of this paper has been the exploitation and exclusion of domestic workers of the informal sector. In this manner increasing poverty among domestic workers hold an important aspect. The articulation of urban poverty is most significant among urban informal workers. It is visible in the work they do, the harassment they face, their conditions of life and work and on their bodies. Not only does their vulnerability of life and livelihood perpetuate their poverty, it also limits access to the benefits designed to give workers stronger bargaining power and assistance in alleviating poverty. More over women remain concentrated in "invisible" areas of informal work, such as domestic labour. It offers precarious employment status, low, irregular or no remuneration, little or no access to social security or protection (Abramo and Valenzuela, 2006).

2.2 Feminisation of Employment VS Feminine Labour: The Feminist Critique

The feminisation of labor force during past decades has intensified the reliance of many women on informalzed employment. Over the past decade in particular, much has been written on the increasing feminisation of the labour force in both developed and developing countries around the world (Standing, 1989; Cagatay and Ozler, 1995; Horton, 1999; Mehra and Gammage, 1999; Ozler, 2000). Guy Standing (1989) has articulated" feminization of employment" in the dual sense of an increase in the numbers of women in the labor force and a deterioration of work conditions (labor standards, income, and employment status). Feminization of labour is the increase in women's share of the labour force. It would seem, therefore, that the continued feminisation of the labour force is associated with rising rates of female unemployment and the feminisation of generally insecure forms of employment. Despite the widespread acceptance that women's presence in the labor market has seen a secular increase in the last few decades, the term 'feminization' itself has been a contentious expression in the literature, perhaps because of its inherent ambiguity. Feminization can refer to three distinct but related processes in the labor market. First, it is sometimes used to simply mean a rise in female labor force participation. A second connotation of the term is the replacement of male workers with (typically cheaper) female workers in various production processes. Finally, feminization is also used to refer to the expansion of employment opportunities with characteristically 'female' traits. Used in this sense, feminization refers not primarily to the gender of the worker, but rather changes in the features of an occupation which may for various reasons also result in an increasing proportion of women in those jobs (Finnoff and Jayadev, 2006). All these changes have also been grouped under the notion of the increased 'flexibilization' or sometimes 'casualization' (Vosko, 2002). Feminine labour has a strong link with the informal labour market (Heintz, 2006). Domestic service is the strong source of feminine labour sector (Pedlar, 1982). Throughout the world, child care and domestic work are considered women's work (Moghadam, 1990). Here understanding the situation of domestic service, informal sector directly connect with the feminisation of labor. Across the globe feminine labor sectors has for more the most part been identified as linked to exploitative conditions, low productivity, low pay (Beneria, 2001). These characteristics of feminine labour sector are as same as the characteristic of informal labour sector. It seems therefore that the continued feminization of the labour force is associated with rising levels of female unemployment and a feminization of low-paid insecure forms of employment. Most of these low paid jobs for women remain in the informal sector. Feminisation of labour in the informal sector also referees the ambiguity of work structures, substantiated by the law; serve to depress wages for the entire unorganized sector. Within this discriminatory scheme of things, feminine labor is routinely under paid. From the context of Bangladesh Domestic, service is the best model of feminization of labor in the informal sector. Since Women, remain over represented in domestic work in the informal sector, work usually seen to have low returns and little security or protection for the worker. Remarkably economic exploitation as well as low payment is the common situation of this sector. Huge numbers of women are involved with the sector who earns a very lower wage in compare to the work time. Another interesting feature of feminine labor sector is high demand for specific categorized women. In some cases, it is women's status as unmarried and subordinate "daughters" that makes them an attractively cheap and flexible pool of labor (Drori, 2000). In other contexts, it is women's status as wives and mothers that justify their lower wages and limited job security (Kondo 1990, Lamphere 1987, Lee 1998, Roberts 1994). These married women and women with children have more family responsibility compare to unmarried women. Disciplinary strategies may also (and often at the same time) position female workers as sexualized bodies whose subordination is maintained through erotic banter and other forms of sexual harassment (Prieto, 1997). Following this, domestic service is strongly confined in feminine labor sector. Employers prefer women not men for doing their household task and also the women from lower and subordinated class. Unmarried and dependent daughter is highly preferred by the employers as they know these categories women's agency is mostly situated (Rehman, 1992). Rehman (1992) also points out that, The girl domestic labor, for sake of their survival and as a coping strategy, usually trusted the employers as the parsons who might well arrange their marriage in future Historically, in Bangladesh, most women were confined by norms of seclusion to work in and around homesteads, carrying out domestic chores and post harvest activities for themselves or others. Here Purda as seclusion has identified as a major factor of feminization of domestic work in Bangladesh.

Articulating the context of domestic works and feminisation of labour many feminist has criticized the notion of feminisation of employment with flexiblisation. According to them the world of flexible labour, sub-contracting and the process of casualisation raise many other complex issues in the context of "gender" exploitation in global economy. Feminist have indentified the informal sector is one of the most affected areas which even otherwise has been plagued by arbitrary gender discrimination, low wages and lack of job security. .according to Guy Standing (1999) Thus they tend to be recruited into the lowest paying jobs within industries, and tend to be over-represented in part-time, temporary and informal sector employment. The feminisation of these sectors has been directly related to a process of degradation of the jobs that women move into. Women's work is not only characterized by low wages, but poor working conditions, insecure employment contracts and few opportunities for career advancement. This is a situation that has been described as the feminisation of flexible employment. Due to this manner feminist have criticized the recognizasion of women's employment as home workers, domestic workers and in other forms of informal sector employment (which includes workers employed in formal workplace settings who are classified as 'self-employed' or 'contract labour')

2.3 Unequal power relation as a source of exploitation

In last fifty years, in addition to theorizing about gender relation and inequalities, feminist turn their attention to social theories of power. Power is broadly defined as the ability to influence the outcomes of the events (Sanchez, 1988). It can mean something that an actor posses which is valuable in itself. Powerlessness, in turn, is the lack of influence over circumstances. This work has been inspired by the work of Bell Hooks (1984) thought on the concept that the powerless can also be powerful. Hooks articulated that women lie in the powerless group in the society. At the same time women can be powerful also if it examine from the intersectionality lens. The challenges for feminist was to establish a link between gender which proved to be a useful analytical concept for explaining between sexes and powering feminist literature power is often described as top-down. In the gendered power structure, feminist claims male impose power as an attempt to prove them as the dominant authority as women are structurally situated to be dominated in patriarchal system. The traditional definition of power has failed to identify the power relation between two women. This research is sought to address some key analytical concerns to consistently apply a critical perspective which examines situation of female domestic workers. It is also to examine the gendered relations of power, to develop and apply a more "intersectional" approach which analyses the ways in which gender is (re)produced through its interaction with a range of other axes of social differentiation (such as "race", ethnicity, class, sexuality; age; religion; and ability from a methodological perspective). We speak of women as a group. We must also note that women as a group are not homogenous. In the work of Smith Dorothy (1987), she assumes patriarchy as the power relation between men and women. Smith's concept of patriarchy does not explain power differences between different women. Smith also dismisses the concept of agency too quickly because she assume that agency is that power which only men as the part of ruling class is able to experience. Recent feminist debate have explained the theories of power not only as the authority and domination of male because women also a strong agent of patriarchy which is defined as Classic patriarchy. Here women equally impose patriarchal ideologies as well as domination to another woman. The cyclical nature of women's power in the household and their anticipation of inheriting the authority of senior women encourage a thorough internalization of this form of patriarchy by the women themselves (Kandiyoti, 2007). From the situation of domestic service this study is to understand the power relationship between two women.

 Sociologist Judith Rollins (1985) conducted some unique research on the relationships between Domestic workers and female employers. Rollins used a variety of techniques to gather her data. She interviewed domestics and employers, worked alongside domestic workers in the guise of being their "cousin," drew on her own experiences as a worker in a number of settings, and interviewed personnel at agencies dealing with domestic workers (Rollins, 1985). While Rollins discovered a variety of relationships between women employers and their domestics, she found that some overall patterns prevailed. As with earlier discussion of women of the upper class, these relationships shed light on the significance of where one is situated within systems of gender, and economic inequality. Gender is an operative concept that does not mean only relation between men and women also relation between women and women or men and men. Women who are privileged by virtue of their class may dominate over other women who hold subordinate positions within systems of economic inequality. Women may be oppressed by other women. In the context of domestic labor it become clear that women's group are also capable to exercise power and that women some are more powerful than other (Sanchez,, 1995).The issue of violence also discloses the multi-dimensional nature of gender and power relation. In the sector of domestic service women are oppressed by two sided violence. Firstly the physical and psychological violence leads by female employers direct against their female employees and secondly sexual harassment leads male employers.

2.4 Intersectionality, Patriarchy and Agency

I will operationalize this study in relation to the patriarchal household, which is relevant to the Bangladeshi context As Feldman (2001) defines; patriarchy in Bangladesh is a system of gender relations that determines women's physical and social mobility, rights, access to resources. Patriarchy often understood as made up of male domination and privilege, the absence of individual agency and the notion of social regulation as a totalizing project (Cain, Khanam and Nahar, 1979; Adnan ,1990; Feldman, 2001). In Bangladesh Patriarchy describes a distribution of power and resources within families that men maintain power and control of resources and women are powerless and dependent on men (Cain, Khanam and Nahar, 2008). However patriarchal relations should be seen as mediated processes of negotiation which constituted by complex identities and practices rather than by an assumed unitary, dominating force of male power and authority and exclusively female subordination (Kandiyoti 1988,1991; Feldman 1992 ,1993). Kandiyoti has articulated a different lens of patriarchy since it provides a window on how 'patriarchy is negotiated and women's strategies play out in the context of patriarchal bargains that act as implicit scripts and prescriptions that highlights their domestic options''(1988). However intersectional lens challenge the conventional theory on patriarchy which have articulated women as a homogenous group of oppressed. The notion of Intersectionality challenges the notions of layers of oppression and discrimination. The discourse of experiences makes Intersectionality, which is one of the indispensable contributions of feminism, to emerge as a significant tool of analysis as well as normative theoretical argument (Hancock, 2007:63). Mohanty (1991) who criticizes the homogenizing of the 'third world' women by sticking to the patriarchal lens to evaluate their experiences without considering the temporal dimensions.

> 'The notion of a road map of a busy town illustrates the meaning of the Intersectionality of oppression and discrimination. There is Racism Road, Patriarchy Parade, Sexism Street, Colonization Crescent, Religious Persecution Road, and Indigenous Dispossession Highway, Class Street, Caste Street, and so on. The road is full of heavy speeding traffic, and the impact of Intersectionality is when a woman from a marginalized group tries to cross the main intersection. To use this model as an analytical tool, we must unpack each of the 'road names' to explore the origin of the oppressions, and the impact of these on women across a range of situations'' (Bartolomei et al., 2003:89).

Theorizing of Intersectionality is the realization that race, color, class, sexuality, nationhood and other social relations of power are equally significant for identities of women, for the process of becoming a woman. By bringing the intersectional analysis as an approach, the research will focus on the intersection of class, gender, age all of which are power relations to define the experiences of women within the acknowledged gender category. In this study patriarchy is defined as a system where not only men but also women exercise the power. By bringing intersectional lens here women have defined as a category of class and sex. Intersectionality attends segregate identities and move to process of exclusion based on context and dynamics of cross-cutting identities (Davis.K; Forthcoming).

In this study intersection analysis are focused on two women in the household setting. This study will analyze how social practices embodied in the intersection of gender, class calls into question that patriarchy as the regular dominant form of social ordering. The main purpose here is to highlight how these differences combine to create women as what Makkonen defined as 'a minority within minority' (2002). In Brah's view different groups of women are situated in different context. Differences in gendered power relations, structures and processes are the ground of this study. Here Domestic service involves a female-to female relationship between a middle- to upper-class employer and a working-class woman, (Chang, 2000; Hondagneu, Sotelo, 2001). Domestic service has been a contentious issue for feminist scholars for it demonstrates power differentials among women. Women of the middle and upper class may tolerate gender dominance in relationships with their husbands. However, their class allows them to dominate certain other persons both male and female within their households such as domestic workers. It challenges essentialist conceptions of gender and of universal womanhood since "many women employers simply perpetuate the sexist division of labor by passing on the most devalued work in their lives to another woman-generally a woman of class" (Romero 1992, 131). Yet domestic service is also an institution through which gender ideology and sexual inequality operate. Intersectionality attends segregate identities and move to the process of exclusion based on context and dynamics of cross- cutting identities (Davis .K:Forth coming).The notion of Intersectionality challenges the notions of 'layers of oppression' and 'discrimination'. This concept suggests that it should be possible to separate the layers out and address the issues one by one. Multiple discriminations based on different grounds at different times, where intersectional discrimination refers to the intersection of discrimination based on several grounds at the same time (Mackinnon, 2002). In this study domestic service cross cut both class and sex. Here patriarchy is understands as the system of power relation between two women from two social-economical grounds is found. The poor women domestic worker is in weak bargaining position compared to employer who is also a woman. Here, gender and class differences are played out through the subordination of one group of women by another, blurring the fact that both experience subordination within the system of gender inequality.

Agency is also linked with issues of different categories women. Agency is an important aspect of intersectional analysis. The concept of agency is also used to characterize an active and deliberate role for participants in the discourse of domestic service. In this study intersectional analysis focuses on the interconnection between power and agency. Harre (1984) suggests that when individuals have agency, they conceive of themselves as having the power to decide, to act independently, and to account for their actions. To have agency means that one speaks and acts from a legitimate position that is prior and separable from the particular discourse of interest. Focusing on informality in the context of employment gives a wider role to agency factors, which will prove a more helpful context in which to examine gender issues, and opens a wider policy agenda in extending socio-economic protection to domestic workers. Negotiation is a key factor of agency exercise among the labor and employer. Negotiators representing two people meet to reach an agreement between them, (Putnam, 1988). Patriarchal bargain is an enormous concept that also refers the capacity to exercise agency. These patriarchal bargains exert a powerful influence on the shaping of women's gendered subjectivity and determine the nature of gender ideology in different contexts (Kandiyoti, 1988) .Women seems to realize lower returns to their salary negotiation efforts (Gerhart and Rynes, 1991). Perhaps it is because they lack confidence in their negotiating abilities (Stevens et al., 1993). It also may be they devalue their contributions and, therefore, seek less pay (Major et al., 1984) because they communicate lower pay expectations, they are offered less. Not surprisingly I find in salary negotiation research that women use fewer self-promotion tactics and, hence, come away with lower pay, are less persistent (Renard, 1993), and set lower salary goals. In the world of negotiation analysis, bargaining power is important. The bargaining approach provides a useful framework for the analysis of gender relation. One's low position in a social hierarchy and a history of dependence on others can translate into psychological feelings of weakness and dependency (Miller, 1976). Domestic worker stays below in the scale of power relation between employers and employee. Their agency is situated. Women working as domestic workers belong to poor household. They are almost bounded to work here as their parents are unable to bear them. These situations take way their agency. They fail to bargain for better wage and working condition. Additionally Bing a wing of informal sector domestics workers do not hold any contract paper or legal documents for the recruitment of the domestic workers. In that case it is very difficult to organize the workers for the purposes of increasing their bargaining power and it illustrate that having no contract paper it is difficult to claim one employer responsible for protecting workers right of domestic workers (Beneria 2001). Both class and sex play the game here. For example, domestic workers are might identify with the high social status of their employers and use it to draw a line between themselves and domestic workers working for employers with a lower social status. More over being poor they are also the female labor force in the informal labor market that reinforces the lower agency in to bargain for labor right and required and valid wage.

CHAPTER THREE: UNDERSTANDING LABOR EXPLOITATION IN HOUSEHOLD SETTING.

As the theoretical framework of the present study demonstrated the financial insecurity and economical exploitation as the major hurdles that domestic workers face as being a worker of the informal labor market. The major findings of the research are also presented in terms of these insecurity, exploitation and disadvantages experiencing by the female domestic workers in Dhaka

3.1 Presenting data on domestic workers

Before going to the main part of the findings, I shall briefly discuss some responses stated by the employers of the domestic workers. In Bangladesh domestic service is a common culture.

This section of informal sector is strongly dominated by women. The unregulated arrangement of the sector produces employer's exploitation over the workers. Most of the domestic workers stated their exploitative situation. This research shows this deregulation as the main source of their exploitative situation.

Operationalsing the framework developed in chapter 2, I use the following eight indicators for the investigation of the labour exploitation in the domestic service.

1. Do the domestic workers hold any formal contract letter?
2. How do they negotiate their salary?
3. Does their work structure matches with their salary and age?
4. What is the Employer's way of approaching to them?
5. Does their identity changes?
6. Do they enjoy any leisure time and holiday?
7. Do they have the freedom to leave the work?
8. Do they experience any incident of Violence and sexual harassment?

3.2 Employer's perception towards domestic work

Hasina Rahman, aged 35, a housewife living in Dhanmondi belief that salary does not mean everything. Her belief is that, her Domestic worker is getting free accommodation and food so Salary should not be must. She states it in the following way.

> *Salary is not everything. What ever I do not give her any salary. I will give this money during her marriage we have decided to bear the whole expense for her marriage. I think I am justifying with her. These plans are for the betterment of her life. We have brought her in her early childhood when she was four years old. However, we do not give her salary. I don't think she is a domestic worker. We treat her like our daughter. She calls us Ma (mother) and Baba (father). I do not think this is a matter of law and regulation. I am helping her family. I have brought her from my village. Here government can not say anything.*

Above case shows, they have hired a domestic worker, when the worker was only four years old. They have hired as a domestic worker but do not give any salary for her labour. She also justified herself. Here most interestingly poverty becomes a strong factor. As the worker is poor and vulnerable the employer thinks she is not exploiting rather she is helping the girl by giving free food and accommodation. She also views this as her personal matter not a matter of government. Nargis Sultana is another housewife, aged 40, expressed her view towards the salary of her domestic help like following manner:

> *I have hired a girl for doing my household task. She is 13 years old. I give her 500 taka every month. They are very poor and her uncle has given her to me. He said to give her 800 Taka. I did not agree with that. She is not that much capable to get more money for this type of work. She does nothing except help me in some simple task. I think her salary is perfect for this type of work. Additionally sometime, her uncle demands money without any reason. Therefore, I have to give money to him also.*

This statement shows that employers (housewife) think that she is justifying with the salary of her domestic worker. She thinks her domestic helper is a child and can not do anything. This is the reason that she have decided to give her 500 Taka for each month. These interviews show that employers are trying to hire domestic worker without salary or with very poor salary. These Employers think that, hiring workers without salary or with 500 Taka monthly is justified for this type of home based labour. Another woman named Sharmin, aged 32, an employee in B.B.C Bangladesh, thinks similarly

> *Yes her salary is ok for this type of job. I am giving her 800 TK. I think this is very justified this is not any hard job. They are taking food and shelter here. They are getting a very comfortable life. If I would not hire her, she would work in another place. Here she is given a good environment. I am not wrong. I had asked their expectation then it matches my expectation then I have decided her salary.*

Here the question arises to what extend employers recognize domestic service as a work. Employers think this is not any job as the workers are staying in a home with a family. It is also true that domestic service is still excluded from labour legislation act of Bangladesh. This exclusion also gives the chance to the employer to exploit their domestic workers. Hasina Rahman, aged 35, gave a contradictory view towards her domestic worker. She stated like following manner:

> *Kulsum, my domestic worker does the household tasks. I remain very busy with my children so she manages every thing. From cooking to*

cleaning she does every thing. I do not treat her as domestic worker. She is like my daughter Here she is staying as a family member which is more than a worker. Domestic workers are already in a higher status. They live a comfort life moreover their demands are increasing day by day. I don't think they need any law and regulation. They are already benefited but yes, well they need a contract paper from where we can know their real address because in some cases domestic workers are thief.

This interview shows that, employer's observation towards domestic worker is very much contradictory. Firstly she said she remain very busy with her children so her domestic worker manages the household tasks. Suddenly she stated that she do not treat Kulsum as a domestic worker. In one hand employers want to say that she treats her as a family member not as a domestic worker. On the other hand she orders the domestic workers to manage all household tasks, even she think her domestic helper may be a thief. She wants a contract paper where there will be the addresses of the domestic worker. Here she is in a doubt that her domestic worker could be a thief whom she was saying her daughter. Naila Ajim, aged 43, is a service holder, who belief that she have a responsibility towards her domestic worker, states it in following manner.

I do not give her any salary. My domestic worker is now 13 years old. She is staying here from 6 years. We have decided to give her marriage with a person who works in abroad. We want her to live with us even after her marriage. His husband will live in abroad and she will live with us

This statement shows that these types of employers have an exploitative view and strategies towards the domestic worker. They are adopting the domestic worker in a broader scale. They want to keep their domestic workers for whole life. They want to arrange the marriage of her domestic worker in a manner that she can keep the domestic worker for whole life. Employers have an authoritative attitude towards the domestic workers. They view this issue as a personal matter. Domestic workers are depriving from a justified wage. In some case they are working without wage. The first thing arises from this data raises the question how these factors creates the exploitation and how the domestic workers view this situation.

3.3 Do not hold any formal contract letter: Domestic workers do not hold any contract paper. There is no formal paper as a security of their job. It promotes employer's unitary authority over the workers. A domestic worker aged 17, states that

> *Yes we are worker .we also need a contract paper. Where our salary,*
> *our age, and also the types of work will be defined*

The above statement shows that contract paper play an important role in every employment. Contract paper can protect labour right. A domestic worker can protest any type of violation through her contract paper. In the sector of domestic service there is no regulation of contract paper that it gives a space to the employers exploit them.

3.4 Negotiation with payment: In response to the question of wage and salary structure most of the domestic worker declared that they do not get any salary. They are working without salary. That mean unpaid labour is a important aspect of this sector. Employers have justified them self by saying that they will give a big amount of money during her marriage. One domestic worker Kulsum, aged 16 said that:

> *They have brought me from my village. After my mother's death my*
> *father got second marriage. My step mother enforced my father to send*
> *me to Dhaka to work and earn for them but I do not get any salary. My*
> *employers have decided to bear the whole expense for my marriage.*
> *Therefore, they do not give me any salary.*

Most of the girl said that, their employer would give some money during their marriage. However, there is no written document of it. Even some time Kulsum,s father demands some money but the employer says they will give the money during her marriage, not now. Here this girl has failed to exercise her agency to negotiate the salary. While she is very poor and also excluded from family, her intersectional identity makes her more vulnerable. She is in the most exploited situation. In another interview a domestic worker aged 14 year, stated that she do not know the amount of her salary.

> *My Mama (uncle) has brought me there. I do not know the amount of*
> *my salary. Even my mother does not anything about my salary. My*
> *mama has decided every thing. He comes here to collect my salary.*

This shows that domestic workers are brought by their relative like uncle and aunty. In this case most of the girls do not know their salary. I think this is a root aspect of economical exploitation that a worker does not no her salary. Here another domestic worker aged 13 also stated similarly.

> I don't know how my salary is. I have not bargain for anything. My
> khala (aunty) have brought me here she know every thing. I never get
> my salary in my hand. Usually my khala (aunty) comes here and takes
> the salary from my khalamma (mistress/employer).

These interviews show that the domestic workers never get the salary on their own hand. They have no access to their income. They even not know the amount of their salary. Here the question arises that to what extent these girls working as domestic workers can negotiate and bargain for the wage of their labour.

3.5 Volume of work structure with their wage and age: The work structure of any employment should be according to the wage and time duration of the job. Here the most special fact is that the any kind of work structure should be justified with the age of the employee. In response of this question one girl aged 16, she explained her horrible experiences

> I don't know when I have become a domestic worker. I can not
> remember because I was only four years old when my madam brought
> me from my village. Now I am 16 years old. I have been working here
> for 12 years. I do not get any salary from them. I do all the household
> tasks. To complete this works I have to wake up at 6 am in the morning
> when all the member of the family are in sleep. I go to bed at 12 pm
> after all of them.

This above case shows that she has been bought as a domestic worker in very early childhood. She was only four years that time. She used to do the entire household task. She wakes up before every one and goes to sleep after everyone. Moreover she is not given any salary in returns of this kind of day-night labour.

3.6 Way of approaching to domestic workers: Taramon a domestic worker, aged 16 stated that she has become used to with this offence. Everybody of the family uses slang languages with her. She said in the following manner:

Sometime they do not call by my name. They use to call me as son of
beach. They often use this when they order something. I have to wake
up before everyone. If one day I become late they use these slang. Even
the children of the house use this to me

This above statement shows that domestic workers are living in a horrible life. They are more vulnerable then the other categories labor of informal sector because they are living in the house of the employer. Here the level of exploitation becomes double.

3.7 Their identity changed through changing their name: Most interesting factor I found is that some of this domestic worker's name has been changed. One girl, aged 16 years said that her name has changed. She stated that

I don't know why this has happened. My real name is Taramon, but
after entering here they have changed my name. Now they call me
"Moon". I actually do not know why this happen to me.

The above interview show that the identity of these workers changed. Employers change their name. They give a modern name to the domestic worker that actually matches with the class of the employer. Another girl named Ratna states another interesting thing. She said

My name was Ratna which matches with the name of my employer's
one of the sister. They were not comfortable with my name. Then they
have changed my name and give a new name. Now my name is Sonia.

This interviews shows that employer always view the discourse of domestic work as a subject of lower class. They feel uncomfortable even the name of a lower classes girl matches with them.

3.8 No scope for leisure time and holiday: Kulsum, aged 16 years, a domestic worker living in Dhanmondi in her employer's house. She has no time for rest and recreation. She stated it in following way

I work the whole day especially from the breakfast to lunch time. I never
get any break or rest. I feel very tired at afternoon. My whole body feels
very exhausted and sleepy. But I can not go for sleep because every
afternoon I have to play with the children of my employer. I never enjoy

28

any holidays as yearly or monthly. Still now I have not visited my home
for a single time am working here from 12 years.

The above case shows that girls are pushed from village even in very early age as she was only 4 year. Here these things become very clear that in some cases these domestic workers are forced.

Even domestic service is also perpetuating child labour. The informal structure of the domestic service support child labour. Moreover they do not get any rest or leave. This is also a characteristics perpetuating in the informal labour market. Most of the time, they feel exhausted and tired. There is no regulation for time to take rest or leave. A girl named khaleda, aged 13, working in the home situated in Dhanmondi also sates similarly. She said that

I never enjoy any holidays as yearly or monthly. From the period, I
have come here, I work whole day. Specifically I work from 8 am to 12
p.m. even if I finish my work quickly I can not go to sleep. I sit and take
rest.
I do not get enough holidays. I only visit my home during Eid. Even few
days ago my sister has born but still now I have not seen her.

This interviews shows that domestic service is a filed of informal employment where there is no regulation for rest and leave. As they belong to the informal sector they have no protective regulation and legislation. They do not receive justified wage moreover they are exploited there. Another girl named Nobu, aged 16 years old, a domestic worker in Dhanmondi also stated her situation as following manner.

All the time I works but they do not see it they only beat me everyday. I
am mentally frustrated, all the time I live in a fear. I feel very bad when
I remain sick. Then I think to have a leave from work. This is not
possible in reality. I have to finish all my work even if I am sick.

This shows that these kind of domestic workers are under an authoritative cage. They are excluded from labour law they easily become the victim of the exploitation of their employers. They are almost a forced labour. Due to poverty they are sent there. They can not go back to their parents. Even they are not permitted to go to village. Because the employers remains in tension that, the worker will not back again. Actually they are trapped in an exploitative labour relation.

3.9 No freedom to leave the work: Domestic service is a sector of high level of labour exploration. A labour should have the right to leave the work if they want. It is very interesting that most of the domestic workers want to leave their work, but they can not do it. Their employer forces them to work here. Moreover employers do not want to increase their salary. Some cases have also showed the situation of the domestic workers who are working without salary. Most of the girl wants to get rid of this exploitation. In an interview, a domestic worker named kulsum, aged 16 stated that

> *I don't want to work here any more. I am tired I am exhausted. Almost everyday I am beaten by my Ma (mistress). I call them Baba and Ma (Father-Mother) but all this relation are fake. This relation is not real. I am only a servant here. They need a slave and I am bound to stay here because we are very poor, I am not accepted to my step mother's family. I can not go back to my parents.*

Another domestic worker working in Dhanmondi, aged 14, also stated similarly. She explained that she is a forced labour. She had no intention to work here. She is totally alienated from her work. She had tried to leave her job for several times.

> *I don't want to work here .this time when I will go to my village in the Eid vacation I will not come here again. I want to get rid of it. I feel so sad. I do not want to stay there anymore .I can not talk to my mother over phone. Madam does not give me the phone whenever my mother calls me from village. One day my mother had called me over phone, but madam said Hamida is not available now, she is sleeping. But I was making ruti (kind of cake) that time. She told lie to my mother.*

3.10 High level of insecurity, Violence and harassment: In urban areas of Bangladesh, women working in household often become victim of violence and maltreatment. Ironically, some housewives despite being women take the lead in committing this act. In response to the question of violence and harassment most of the domestic workers declared that more or less they are victim of it. Here I found the most intersecting things. I found that intersection between class and sex. Here I found the power relation between two face to face women that challenges the traditional meaning of gender and power relation. Most of the domestic workers declared that they are oppressed and subjugated by the female employers. Beating and slapping is the common experience for them. One of the domestic workers, aged 16 year stated that:

> *Often I am beaten by my madam (female employer). Whole day I work*
> *for her. She is not satisfied. She beats me and says that I am destroying*
> *her life and I do nothing. Whole day I take rest*

Interestingly this case shows that female employers are oppressing another categorized powerless woman while they are also the powerless group under their husband. I found the interesting things that domestic workers are physically oppressed by the female employers. Female employers slap and beat their domestic worker. In that case while the question of male employer arises it shows that domestic workers are sexually harassed and abused by them. In one hand they are beaten by the female employer on the other hand they are sexually harassed by the male member of the household. Kulsum, aged 16, working in Dhanmondi explained that she is harassed by the men whom she calls Baba (father). He is her employer. She stated in following manner:

> *I call him Baba (father). He often tries to talk to me alone and suggests*
> *me not to share this with her wife. However, my mother (mistress) is*
> *already known to this relation. Sometime Ma (Mistress), becomes so*
> *angry and crazy that she shouts and says "happy wedding....happy*
> *wedding... of my husband and the bride is kulsum, my made servant.*

Domestic service is held inside the household. This job has become a place of multi faces exploitation. Most of the girls are victim of high level of violence and insecurity. Another girl named Nobu, aged 16, said about her horrible experiences. She shared me the situation like this way:

> *I often sexually harassed by the son of my employers who is 25 years*
> *old. This man comes to me when I am alone in the home. Often he tries*
> *to touch me and request me to come to his bed room and massage his*
> *body. These things make me vary frustrated. Even I never share this*
> *with my madam. Her parents are totally unknown to this offence. We*
> *are working here. We are treated like a servant, slave. What ever they*
> *do not give me salary moreover the beat me, harass me. But I can not*
> *do anything. I can not go back to my parent's home. They are very*
> *poor. They can not bear me. I know I am bound to stay here for whole*
> *life.*

Here intersection between class and sex reinforces the exploitative situation. Men found female domestic worker as a subject to sexual harassment because they are powerless in two sides. Firstly they belong to female sex secondly they also belong to lower class.

3.11 Worker's perception toward their work: It is clear that some of the domestic workers are not conscious whether their salary is justified or not. Interestingly most of them think they are exploited in the case of their salary or wage. They think they are cheated, and exploited by their employer. One domestic worker aged 14 year, explained this in following words:

> *I think I should get a better salary. We are poor for that reason I choose to work here. I earn 500 taka each month. Truth is that my mother has said that she can not able to maintain our family with my poor salary. I feel very sad. Some time I think to leave this job and also think to find new job where I can earn more.*

The above fact reveals that domestic worker belief that domestic service a sector where the workers are given very poor wage for heavy hard working. That's why she thinks to leave this work. Here another worker aged 16, working in Dhanmondi also arise this issue from a slight different angle. She claimed her demand of rest and leave.

> *I feel very sad and frustrated because there is no return of my day-night hardworking. Our wage is very poor. I think we should get a better payment. Not only that I want specific time of each day for rest and specialty permission to meet and communicate with my relatives over phone.*

The above statement describes another dimension of exploitation. They are underpaid. Moreover they have no leave, no specific time for rest. Additionally they are totally separated from their relatives. Their work structure does not match with their salary structure. They work whole day but receive a poor wage.

Finding support and confirms that the female domestic workers of Bangladesh are situating in an exploitative situation. Domestic service is a sector of feminised labour. Additionally is a strong branch of informal labour market. This two main factor reinforces various forms of injustice. Injustice in wage is one of the root forms of the exploitation. In fact the empirical data shows that in maximum cases young girls working as a domestic worker do no get any salary additionally they become victim of violence and sexual harassment.

This chapter mainly indicates how the informal nature of domestic service reinforces lower wage and financial insecurity for the domestic workers. It is clear that domestic service a sector of feminine labour. Huge number of women and girls are working but the exploitative labour relation strengthen the under payment for the worker in this sector. The empirical findings show that, the intersection between sex and class ensures the exploitation in different way. Here lower class women are oppressed by the higher class women. Here class plays the most interesting game. The informal nature of their work reinforces the exploitation and their class reinforces the lower agency. For that reason I found domestic service as a sector where the agency of domestic workers is not only situated but also exploited.

By considering the above cases, we can claim the domestic service, as branch of informal sector creates unlimited labour exploitation. Material dependency explores that domestic service is situating in a setting of unfairness toward the workers which produces and integrates injustice and exploitation in various way. The explanation of various factors of domestic service will address the main research question, which is, What are the strategies and factors by which informal sector promotes exploitation among female Domestic workers?

3.12 Intersectionality and the difference experiences of female domestic worker

By analyzing the above interviews I have found that that domestic service is a strong platform of exploitation on women. Most of the Women view it as a sector of employment. Hence this study unveils that domestic service is obviously an employment sector for women. As Huge number of poor women works in this sector. However at the same time it creates high level of exclusion for poor women. Poor women join an employment to reduce their poverty but this sector do not reduces poverty furthermore it creates exploitation and insecurity. The factors associate with the reason of exploitation is multi faced. There are the factors of class, sex, age in the axis of the platform of the domestic service. Applying intersectional approach it has came out that domestic service is a section where gender is (re) produced through its interaction with a range of other axes of social differentiation such as class, sexuality; age. By applying the intersectional lens this study has identified five factors which make them more vulnerable.

Gender: an axis of social relation

Gender inequality is a salient feature in different aspects of Bangladesh, and it is considered as critical in labour market due to the significant role in influencing the participation of women in economic, social and political spheres of the country. By applying the intersectional lens this study has indentified gender as an axis of discrimination. This study shows that women are over represented in the informal sector. Not only that this study has show that, gender makes a strong segmentation in the informal sector. In the theoretical chapter it has been make clear that women tend to be predominant in the lower status job of the informal sector. In the context of Bangladesh, different research shows that almost 80% employee of domestic service are women who are from lower class. Here employers can exploit the employee for two reasons because they are from informal sector. Secondly they are women also from poverty. Poor women have the lowest capacity to exercise their agency. It gives the employers to dominate the employee.

Social class: as an axis of Social Relation

Another important factor I have found that in the domestic service the social class plays an important role. This study shows that domestic service is a sector where both the employee and the employer are women. Here two women remain in a face to face relation. From the intersectional analysis this research explores that here the power relation exist between the same sexes. Here their sex is same but their class is not same. The employer is the upper class women while the employee is from the lower class background. Here the one woman can dominate another woman because class allows the employer to stay in the higher position. It perceives that female domestic workers are under the authority of uppers class female employer. Hence In the first barging table domestic workers fail to exercise their agency before the upper class employer.

Classic patriarchy: as an axis of discrimination

Intersectionality gives this study a different shape through which this study challenges the tradition meaning of gender. It had assumed that gender is the relation between men and women. Due to this the patriarchy was assumed as the rule of the father where male dominate women though this study shows that in the patriarchy not only men also women dominate women. That is said the "classic patriarchy", where women exercise her power on another women. In the domestic service the domestic workers works under the authority of a women. It pushes her to be dominated by another woman. Most interestingly in this section woman fails to use their agency before another women. The intersectional approach explains that both of this two sided women employer and employee are women. The research shows that their sexual identity is same but here the class and age works as an indicator of dominating power relation. Domestic workers are belongs to lower class additionally they live in the home of the employer. They fail to bargain with upper class. Evidence from the study indicates that these intersectional factors ensure the subordinated position of domestic workers. Here they are subordinated to another woman. Here domestic workers agency is not only situated it is exploited also.

Age: as an axis of exploitation

This study shows age as an important factor for domination and exploitation. Age is an important factor for agency. A Woman's agency is formed by her age. Here I vane found that the lower aged domestic worker's agency is also lower than the higher aged worker. In mu study I have found that a domestic workers name d Khaleda, aged 13 never raise her voice to protest the over exploitation to her whether another girl Nobu, aged 16 said that she tries to protest these offence. Here Khaleda is younger than Nobu. Her age makes her more vulnerable and inferior in comparison to another girl who is elder than her. Even this study also discovers that all the employers are above 30 year, where all the domestic workers are below 20. Here the most interesting things the research shows that age can be a major tool of domination. In the one hand all the domestic workers are from lower class one the other hand they are also lower aged than the employer. Here age also becomes a major factor with class.

Language: as an axis of identity crisis

In this research it has identified language as an axis of subordination. One can be dominated by language as well as by the way of approaching. Interestingly in this study explores that in some cases the name of the domestic workers has been changed after joining the job. They are not called by their real name. Employers give them new and modern name. Moreover Domestic workers are often verbally abused by the employers. Even they are treated with slang language. These push them in an inferior and subordinated status.

Sexuality as an axis of violence

Hence, in this research, sexuality is considered as social relation, in whom these five elements are manifested in one or another way and the underlying concern to deal with the issue is that the need of looking at sexuality as significant social reality that shape the experiences of girls beyond as subjective matter.

This study perceives informal sector as well as the structure of the informal sector as the main source that produces labour exploitation in domestic service. There is no legal protection and formal regulation in the informal sector which gives the chance to the employers of the domestic service to exploit the domestic workers. Most of the girls working as a domestic service comes form poor household. Here poverty is a push factor. To recover their immediate poverty situation they easily join domestic service. In the context of urban household domestic workers are always demeaned. They join domestic service to remove poverty but in actual they caught in the trap of informal sector. Here they face high level of insecurity with very low level of earnings and unstable working conditions. Evidence from the study indicated that most of the domestic workers have raised the issue of lower earning. Most interestingly some of them are totally unpaid. They stated that their employer have decided to give their wage during their marriage. It perceives that the informal regulation of this sector have given the chance to the employers to exploit the labor like this way. Employers have hired a labor from the labour market but shockingly the labor is unpaid. These exploitative strategies have become possible for the informal characteristics of this sector. This picture clearly states that domestic service creates a vicious circle of poverty. Domestic service as a branch of informal employment includes poor women as a source of employment again it excludes women creating exploitation and insecurity. In this context obviously the informal nature of the domestic service produces the exclusion of female domestic workers.

3.13 Perpetuating injustice in the feminized sector

Throughout the world, child care and domestic work are considered women's work. It perceives Domestic service as a feminized sector of employment that enhance dual sense firstly an increase the numbers of women in the labor force and a deterioration of work conditions (labor standards, income, and employment status). It is also true that Across the globe feminine labor sectors has for more the most part been identified as linked to exploitative conditions, low productivity, low pay (Beneria, 2001). This is a poorly defined occupation which also perpetuates feminisation of labour. This research shows that in Bangladesh there is huge demand for female worker in the domestic sector. In this manner the context of domestic service in Bangladesh has become a discourse of low payment with unlimited injustice. This research shows that Employers have a preconceived belief toward the female domestic workers that they are dependent and helpless. Employers also think that they are helping the domestic workers rather they are exploiting them. The overall analysis shows that employers views domestic service as a working sector of huge number of helpless and vulnerable women. These make factors make them easy to force the domestic workers to stay with the job. The study shows that most of the worker fell alienated from their work. They do not stay here anymore. In most of the cases employer forces them to work. Employer's hierarchal position allowed them to create force on the domestic labor. This experience explores the agency of the employer is higher. That they can keep cheap labor in some cases unpaid labor. These realities reinforce the chance of employers to exploit the domestic workers. However, I want to flag here four sets of relevant findings.

A. The Informal nature of the domestic service produces the platform for exploitation. Lack of regulation and lack Governmental interference promotes the irregular arrangement of the domestic service. This actually creates the space and the sources for employers to do unlimited injustice.

B. Domestic service is a sector that creates vicious circle of poverty for female domestic worker. Poverty includes women in the income generating activity at the same time it excludes them creating labour exploitation including low wage and high level of insecurity. They join here to protest their poverty situation, to remove their poverty situation but interestingly here they can not changes the situation. They was poor they remain poor. Here poverty re-includes them. This is how this research shows the vicious circle of poverty among the female domestic workers.

C. This research shows domestic service as a source of power relation between two face to face women. Through it this study challenges the conventional meaning of gender that referees the power relation between men and women only. This study shows that there are some other factors out of gender. Classic patriarchy becomes an interesting aspect of the findings. Domestic service is a sector where women oppress another woman. Here the upper class woman holds the power and authority to dominate another woman from lower class, who is excluded by her poverty situation.

D. Applying intersectional lens this research has found that gender is not the only factor here class, poverty and age are also a strong factor. I have taken the sample aged 12 to 20 years. This study show that the negotiation power and the capacity to exercise agency is not same for the girl aged 13 and the girl aged 16. Here the intersectional analysis explores that the younger domestic worker have lower capacity to exercise agency than the elder one.

CHAPTER FOUR

4.1 Mapping of social realities:

The labour act of Bangladesh -2006 excludes domestic workers as the labour act was designed specially for the workers of formal labour. They has been excluded and exploited from almost every prohivation of labour legislation because they are women from lower class who performs household in the informal sector. Her work is considered as "women's work or non-work". In finding the dilemmas of female domestic workers in Dhaka, Bangladesh I have noted some recommendations for the policy maker in following way. However, the following guiding principles should be seen as essential aspects of a positive policy process to promote and protect domestic workers from their exploitative situation.

- First of all policy maker should rethink the informal economy to linkage with the formal economy. They should think to formalize the informal sector. Policymakers have tended to over react to the informal economy, trying to discourage it altogether, to treat it as a social problem or to promote it as a solution to economic stagnation or employment creation. It should re think by the policy maker that informal economy is the oft-repeated and greatly-misunderstood question of whether or not to 'formalize' the informal economy.

- Domestic workers should recognize as formal labour and should bring under the protection of law. For example in Bangladesh domestic workers have been excluded from the labour act 2006. This labour legislation has been designed for the formal worker only. It has made them more vulnerable. Due to this vulnerability this research tries to hold serious attention to protect the domestic workers by the labour legislation.

- There is an immediate need of a regulatory for the workers of informal sector. An appropriate regulation can take the workers out of this exploitative situation. In the question of domestic service there should be a strong regulation for both the employer and employee. There should be a contract paper for the recruitment of a domestic worker. Where the age limitation, salary structure, work structure and time limitation of the work should be mentioned. The issue of leisure time and leave should be also mentioned in that contract paper.

- Policy maker should acknowledge the issue that can Protect the domestic worker from economic as well as other exploitation and empower them economically through creating opportunities on education, skill development training.

- To ensure that appropriate policies are put in place, the informal workforce needs to be visible to policymakers. Also, to ensure that the policy approach is well-informed it needs to be evidence-based. Yet there are currently limited data on the informal economy. As During this research I also recognize that there are limited data on the domestic workers. Especially in this sector there is a gap in gender disaggregate data. Greater priority needs to be given to the collection of data on domestic workers, which is a relatively new topic in labour statistics.

- There should be a safe guard of policies and regulation to secure rights of the domestic workers.
    1. Informal wage workers like domestic workers, through extending the scope of existing legislation, promoting collective bargaining agreements and enforcing labour standards.

2. Through which they can build and recognize the 'voice': by joining trade unions, cooperatives, or other membership-based organizations and their representation in relevant policymaking or rule-setting institutions or in collective bargaining agreements.

- Finally, it should be gender sensitive, taking into account the roles and responsibilities of women and men in the informal economy. In most regions of the world, within the informal economy, women tend to be concentrated in lower-return segments than men. As a result, even within the informal economy, there is a significant gender gap in earnings and in the benefits and protection afforded by work.

4.2 TRANSFORMATIVE STRATEGY IN SOCIAL JUSTICE DISCOURSE : UNPACKING THE SOCIAL AND INSTITUTIONAL ARRANGEMENTS

This research explores the circumstances and explains the dilemmas of domestic service in, Dhaka, Bangladesh. Domestic service is a common practice in Bangladesh. Domestic work, being deep-rooted in the Bangladesh society, may not easy to eliminated. This particular service belongs to the informal sector, and is such away from development benefit. This traditional practice in reinforced by extreme poverty also by the socio-economic structure of our society. Especially female domestic workers comes from poor household and with financial pressure at home, have little choice and option. This research shows that female domestic workers in Bangladesh experience a vicious circle of poverty. In this cycle poverty as a key context for poor women includes as well as push them to join the domestic service. After this inclusion they experience a set of exploitation and injustice because of the informal nature of this sector. Which, I think the reproduction of poverty and insecurity. Here the poverty context excludes them from using agency and decision making power also by devaluing their job. Before joining in the domestic service poor women view it as an employment that can take them out of poverty. That, in reality re-include in financial insecurity with high level of exploitation. Ultimately in this context domestic service is shifting the risk of poverty for poor women. They were poor before joining there even still now they remain poor by experiencing high level of exploitation and exclusion. Interestingly, in the context of women and poverty researcher have identified employment as a vehicle to take women out of poverty but this research shows that informal employment as if domestic service never reduces poverty in addition it addition it enhance the process of disempowerment and exploitation .This study draws an outline of the work context of domestic sector by applying intersectional approach. Firstly the workers are women, secondly they perform it in household, thirdly they perform housework, fourthly and most interestingly they perform the work under another woman who belongs to upper class. Most of the researchers identified gender, poverty as the key factor of exploitation on female workers. This study show there are also some other factor like classic patriarchy, age. The

39

number of social power spaces the exclusion experience of domestic workers. Within the authority of employers domestic workers stood in a line of subordination. This system contributes to domestic workers being trapped in abusive situation as some employers may restrict in the domestic setting women stood below her husband and the domestic worker stood below the wife. In this situation their agency is not only situated but also exploited.

The associate reason for the exclusion and omission of domestic service is the social status of the workers and work context of the occupation. Still now domestic service is a sector of feminisation of labour. According to a research done by Save the Children and Ain-O-Shalish Kendra 80% of the domestic workers are female. Even in my research I have not found any male domestic worker in the randomly selected household. Employers have a neglected attitude towards feminine labour. Most of the exclusion happens in the feminine labour sector. In this manner domestic service is still now exclusively performed by the lower class women who are at the same time also the workers of the informal sector. Here the context of feminisation of labour and the informal sector creates the space and the platform for the employers to exploit and exclude the female domestic workers. This research identified the reasons of this exclusion is that they perform housework in a private household, her work contribution is considered minimal, meriting substandard wages, and, most unfortunately until recently, they are excluded from the protective labour legislation.

References:

Beneria, L. (2001) *"Gender, development, and globalization: economics as if all people mattered,"* Routledge publisher.

Charmes, J. (2000) *"Informal Sector, Poverty and Gender: A review of empirical study"* Background paper for the world development report 2001.Washington DC.

Cain, Khanam and Nahar. (1979) *"Class, Patriarchy and Women,s Work in Bangladesh"* Population and Development Review, Vol 5(3) pp.405-38.

Chen, M.A. (2001) *"Women in the informal sector: a global picture, the global movement"*, *SAIS Review*, Winter-Spring 2001.

Chen, M.A.and Lund (2002) *"Supporting workers in the informal economy: a policy framework"*, ILO Employment Sector Working Paper on the Informal Economy, No. 2002/2.

Chang, R.and Culp, Jr. (2002) '*After Intersectionality'* University of Missouri Kansas City Law Review 485-91.

Davis, K. (2008) *"Intersectionality as a buzz word:a sociology of science perspective on what makes feminist theory successful"* in feminist theory, SAGE Publications, Los Angeles.

Dorothy, S. (1987) *"The everyday world as a problematic: A feminist sociology"* Toronto, The University press of Toronto.

Drori, I. (2000) "The *Seam Line: Arab Workers and Jewish Managers in the Israeli Textile Industry"*. Stanford, CA: Stanford Univ. Press

Dalisay S., Sining C. and Aleli R (2009), *"Informal Employment in Bangladesh"* working paper for ADB

Feldman, S. (1992) *"Crisis, Islam and Gender in Bangladesh: The Social Construction of a Female Labor Force"*. In L. Beneria and S. Feldman (eds.) Unequal Burden: Economic crises, persistent poverty and Women's work.

Gerhart, B., & Rynes, S. (1991) *"Determinants and consequences of salary negotiations by male and female MBA graduates"*. Journal of Applied Psychology.

Guy Standing (1989)*"Global* feminization *through flexible* labor*: A theme revisited"*. Journal: World Development Issue.

Harris,White, (2003) *"India Working: Essays on Society and Economy"* Cambridge University Press.

Hart, Keith, (1973) *"Informal Income Opportunities and Urban Employment in Ghana"* Journal of Modern African Studies.

Hart, K. (1970) *"Small- Scale Entrepreneurs in Ghana and Development Planning."* The Journal of Development Studies

Harré, Rom, and Luk van Langenhove (1984) *"Positioning Theory: Moral Contexts of Intentional Action"* Oxford: Blackwell.

Hooks, B. (1984) *"Feminist Theory: From Margin to Center"* South End Press, Boston.

Hossain, M. (2002) *"Child Labour Ternds and Features"*

Heintz, J. (2006). *"Informality, gender, and poverty: a global picture."* Economic and Political Weekly, 41(21): 2131-39

Harding, S. (2005*) "New Feminist Approaches to Social Science Methodologies"* serial publication

Kondo, D. (1990). *"Crafting Selves: Power, Gender, and Discourses of Identity in a Japanese Workplace"* Chicago: University of Chicago Press

Kandiyoti, D. (1998) *"Gender, Power and Consentation: Rethinking bargaining with Patriarchy"* in C. Jackson & R. Pearson (eds.) Feminist Visions of Development: Gender Analysis and Policy, Routledge, London, New York.

Kabeer, N. (2001) *"Bangladesh Women Workers and Labour Market Decisions: The Right to   Choose"*, Vistaar Publications/ Sage, New Delhi.

Kalayaan, (1995) *"Slavery Still Alive."* Justice for Overseas Domestic Workers. Conference Papers, London.

Leslie, G. (1974) *"Domestic Service in Canada 1880-1920"* Women's Educational Press, Toronto.

Moghadam,V. (1990) *"Gender, Development, and Policy: Toward Equity and Empowerment"* World   Institute for Development Economics Research of the United Nations University

Mohanty, C (1991) *"Under Western Eyes: Feminist Scholarship and Colonial Discourses Third World Women and the Politics of Feminism"* Blooming: Indiana university Press.

Momsen, J. (ed. , , 1999) *"Gender, migration and domestic service"* Routledge London.

Miles, A.(1981) *"The Domestic Labour Debate"* Canadian Forum, Vol. 61 PP.36-37.

Mohiuddin .Y (1982) *"female handicraft workers:the invisible hand"*, Pakistan and gulf economist

Romero *M. (,* 1992*) "The Inclusion of Citizenship Status in* Intersectionality*"* Routledge.

Renard, M.K., (1992) *"Salary negotiations and the male-female wage gap."* Unpublished Dissertation, University of Maryland.

Rehman, H. (1992) *"Situation of Child Domestic Servants",*UNICEF, Dhaka.

Rollins, R, (1985) *"Between women"* Philaddelphia, temple universesity press.

Sarkar, S. (2007) *"Gender, Work and Poverty"* Serials Publication, New Delhi.

Smith, D. (1981) *"Women, Class and Family"*, paper presented for SSHRC Workshop on Women and the Canadian Labour Force, U.B.C.

Selim, N. (2009) *"Domestic Service in Bangladesh, a Case Study in Dhaka"* Expressions LTD.Bangladesh.

Shamim, I., Huda, M. N. and Mahmud, S. (1995) *"Child Domestic Work in Dhaka: A Study of the Explotative Situation. Dhaka,"* Save the Children Fund Australia with Anti-Slavery Internationalk, Bangladesh.

Sethuraman, S.V (1998) *"Gender, Informality and Poverty: A Global Review,"* World Bank, Washington, DC.

Pedlar, D. (1982) *"A Study of Domestic Service in Canada"* Research paper university of British Columbia.

Prieto, M. (1997) *"The Discreet Charm of Being Male",* Universidad Complutense de Madrid and Universidad de Barcelona

Putnam, D. (1988). *"Diplomacy and domestic politics: The logic of two-level games"* International Organization 42:427-60.

Appendix A: Questionnaire

Questionnaire for worker

1. Do you know your age? If yes, how old are you?

2. Why you have chosen to work as a domestic helper?

3. When have you entered here?

4. Is it the first time experience of working as the domestic labor?

5. When are the normal hours of your work?

6. When you get up and go to sleep

7. How much is your salary now?

8. How much was your salary when you had joined here?

9. How you had bargain with the employers to fix your salary?

10. When you get it? After each month?

11. Do you enjoy any over time compensation for extra works?

12. Do you have any increment of your salary?

13. Do you think your wage is ok for your work?

14. Do you enjoy any specific time for daily and weekly rest or annual leave?

15. What is your perception on your working situation?

16. How many days you want to work here?

17. Does your employer cut any deduction for destruction of your employer's resources?

18. Do you want to protect your work by national laws and regulations?

19. Do you experience any occurrence of violence or harassment?

Questionnaire for employer

1. What is your occupation?

2. Why you decide to employee fulltime servant?

3. How do you feel to employee a child labor?

4. Do you think there should be a standard rate of remuneration?

5. How do you decide the salary of your domestic helper?

6. Do you think the salary is ok for day and night work?

7. Would you like to give your helper fixed hours of work, overtime compensation?

8. There is no period of daily and weekly rest for them how do you feel?

9. Do you agree that accommodation and food should be safe and decent?

10. Domestic work should protect by national laws and regulations what is your opinion?

11. Should there be any agreement paper for employee a domestic labor?

12. Which type of maid you prefer? educated/good looking

13. Your perception about Domestic workers enjoy at least 24 consecutive hours of rest in every seven day period.

14. Do you cut any deduction for any destruction of your resource by the helper?